POEMS AND PAINTINGS BY

Douglas Florian

Harcourt Brace & Company

SAN DIEGO • NEW YORK • LONDON

INSECTLOPEDIA

Requests for permission to make copies of any part of the
work should be mailed to: Permissions Department,
Harcourt Brace & Company, 6277 Sea Harbor Drive,
Orlando, Florida 32887-6777.

Library of Congress Cataloging-in-Publication Data
Florian, Douglas.
Insectlopedia: poems and paintings/by Douglas Florian.
p. cm.
Summary: Presents twenty-one short poems about such insects as
the inchworm, termite, cricket, and mayfly.
ISBN 0-15-201306-7
1. Insects—Juvenile poetry. 2. Children's poetry, American.
3. Insects in art—Juvenile literature.
[1. Insects—Poetry. 2. American poetry.] I. Title.
PS3556.L589I57 1998
811'.54—dc20 96-23029

C E F D

PRINTED IN HONG KONG

This book is for

Zoe and Rose Birnbaum
Ore, Liane, and Ilil Carmi
Zoe and Victoria Goldenberg
Calla Henkel
Eamon Johnston
Natanel, Elinore, and Dorine Lallouche
Chaya, Beila, and Sarah Leboeuf
Moshe and Maya Madjar
Molly McTague
Dafna, Adam, and Chaya Mushka Mendelson
Stephanie, Ian, Rebecca, and Vaughn Pfeffer
Ariel and Michael Podwal
Emily and Michael Theodore

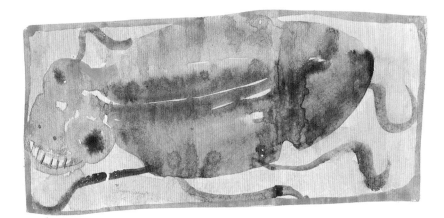

Contents

THE CATERPILLAR

She eats eight leaves at least
To fill her,
Which **leaves** her like a
Fatterpillar,
Then rents a room inside
A pupa,
And checks out: Madame Butterfly—
How super!

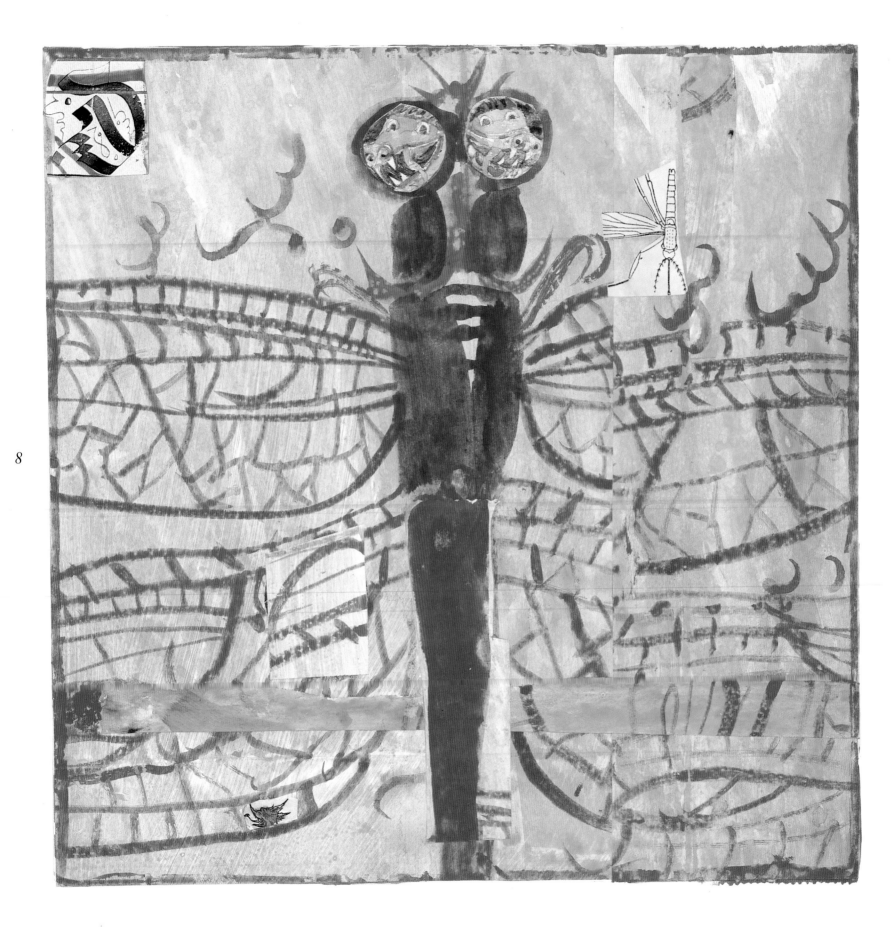

THE DRAGONFLY

I am the dragon,
The **demon** of skies.
Behold my bold
Enormous eyes.
I sweep
      I swoop
            I terrorize.
For lunch I munch
On flies and bees.
Mosquitoes with
My feet I seize.
I am the dragon:
Down on your knees!

THE DADDY LONGLEGS

O Daddy
Daddy O
How'd you get
Those legs to grow
So very long
And lean in size?
From spiderobic
Exercise?
Did you drink milk?
Or chew on cheese?
And by the way,
Where are your knees?
O Daddy
Daddy O
How'd you get
Those legs to grow?

10

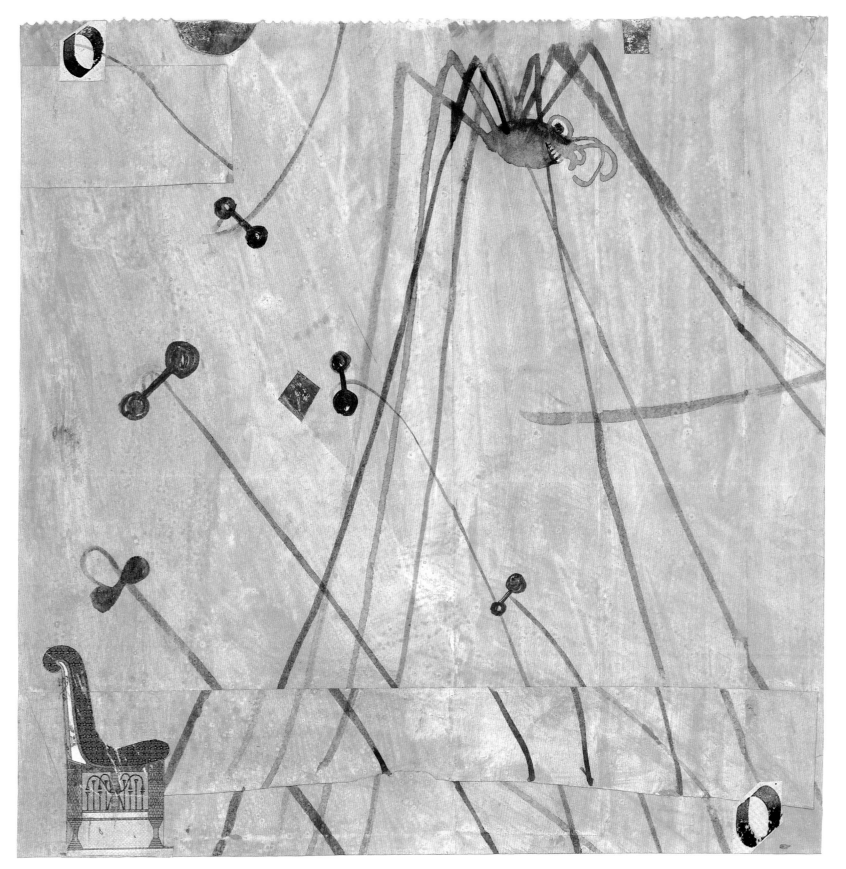

THE ARMY ANTS

Left

         Right

Left

         Right

We're army ants.

We swarm.

    We fight.

We have no home.

We roam.

We race.

You're lucky if

We miss your place.

THE INCHWORM

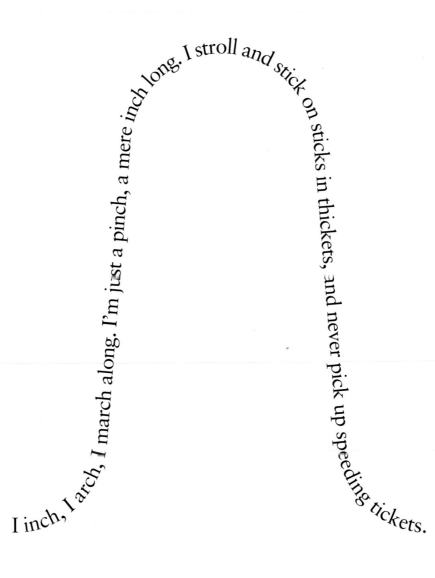

I inch, I arch, I march along. I'm just a pinch, a mere inch long. I stroll and stick on sticks in thickets, and never pick up speeding tickets.

THE PRAYING MANTIS

Upon a twig
I sit and pray
For something big
To wend my way:
A caterpillar,
Moth,
Or bee—
I swallow them
Religiously.

THE BLACK WIDOW SPIDER

I am a widow—
I always wear black,
From my eight dainty legs
To my shiny round back.
Do not disturb me.
My fangs carry venom.
I am a widow—
I don't wear blue denim.

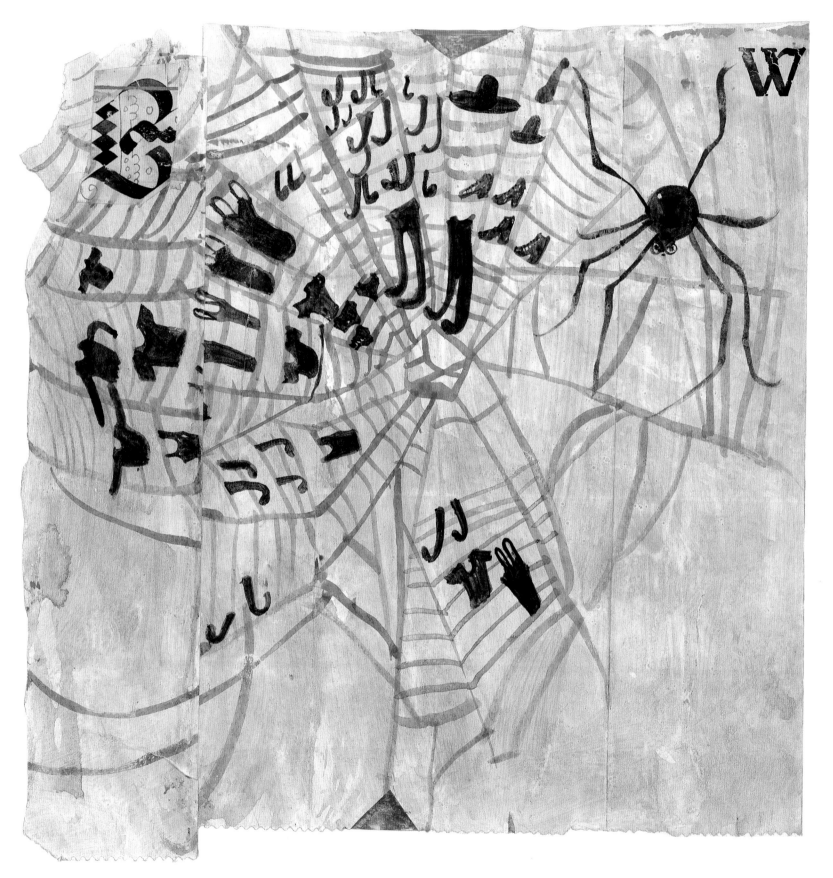

19

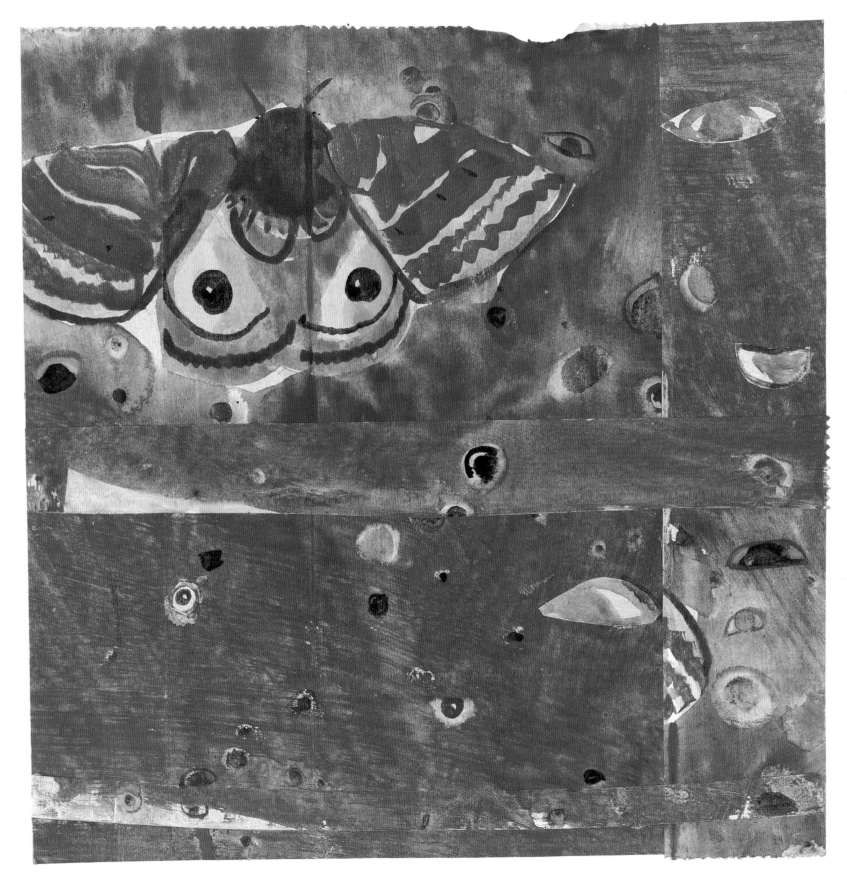

20

THE IO MOTH

The io moth
Has mam-moth eyes
That are not real—
They're a disguise
To ward off birds
And other creatures,
Like garter snakes
And science teachers.

21

THE WHIRLIGIG BEETLES

                            We
            noise.   whirl,
        or   we
        keys   twirl,
        windup   we
        the   skate,
        without   we
        toys,   glide.
        little   Upon
        like   a
        circles   pond
            in   or
            swim   lake
                We   .ride   we

23

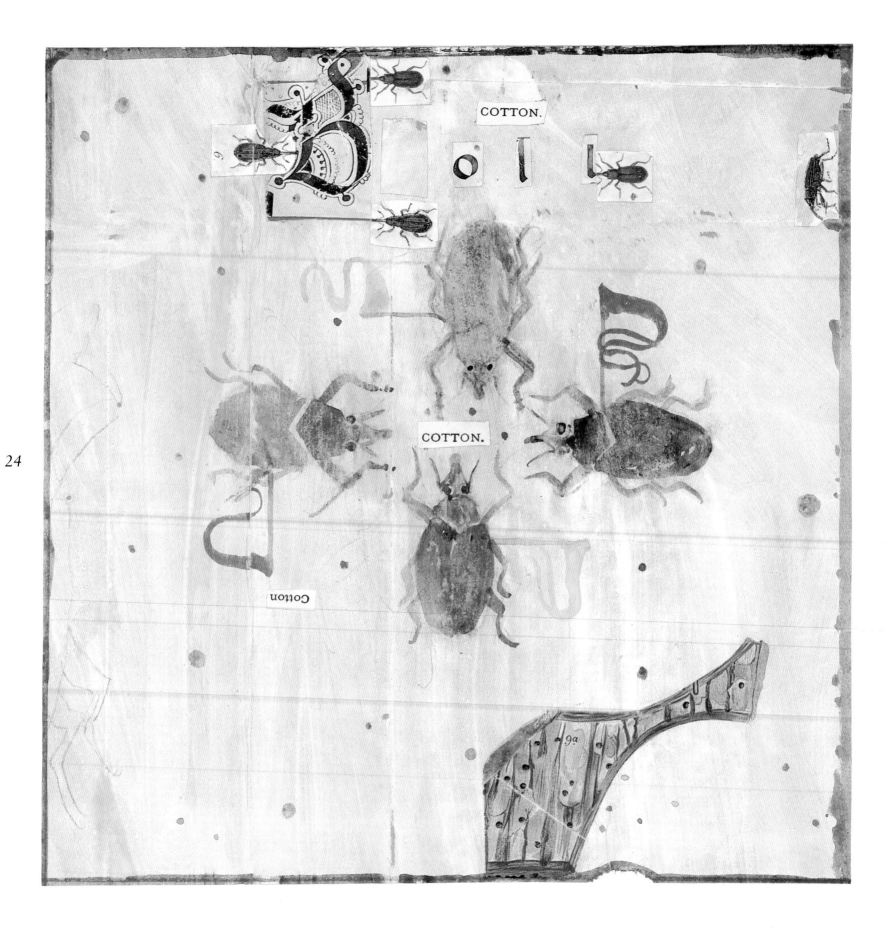

24

THE WEEVILS

We are weevils.
We are evil.
We've aggrieved
Since time primeval.
With our down-curved
Beaks we bore.
Into crops
And trees we gore.
We are ruinous.
We are rotten.
We drill holes
In bolls of cotton.
We're not modern,
We're medieval.
We are weevils.
We are evil.

THE WALKINGSTICK

The walkingstick is thin, not thick,
And has a disappearing trick:
By looking like a twig or stalk,
It lives another day to walk.

27

28

THE HORNET

A hornet's born with yellow rings
Ending in a point that stings.
She builds a pulpy paper nest,
In which few choose to be a guest.
A hornet is an insect killer—
She feeds her babies caterpillars,
Spiders, flies, and if she's able,
Pudding from your picnic table.

THE TREEHOPPERS

They're hip.
They hop
On top of trees.
They skip
On tips
Of twigs
With ease.
They lunge.
They plunge.
They lurch.
They lope.
Imagine what
They'd do
With rope!

O

H

P

31

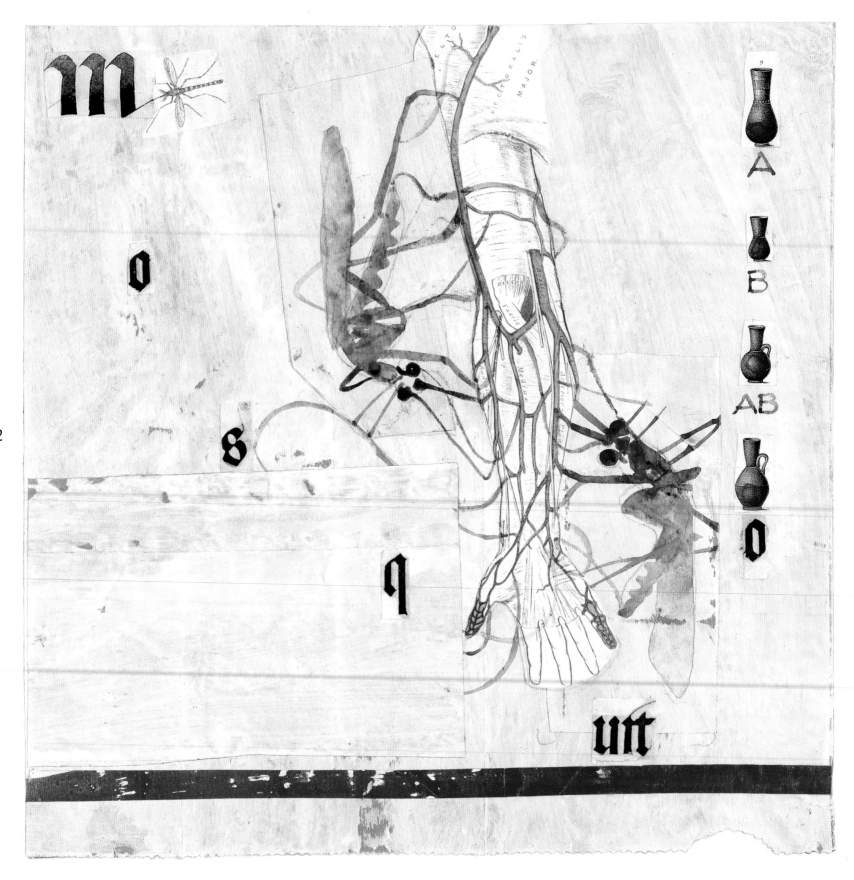

THE MOSQUITOES

Mosquitoes are thin.
Mosquitoes are rude.
They feast on your skin
For take-out food.

33

The Monarch Butterfly

He is a monarch.
He is a king.
He flies great migrations.
Past nations he wings.
He is a monarch.
He is a prince.
When blackbirds attack him,
From poison they wince.
He is a monarch.
He is a duke.
Swallows that swallow him
Frequently puke.

prince

The Giant Water Bug

The giant water bug can lug
His eggs upon his back.
He gives them extra care up there
And guards them from attack.
The mother glues them to the dad,
And on his back they stay.
But does he ever get a card
Or gift for Father's Day?

THE TERMITES

Our
high and
mighty
termite
mound
arises
far above
the ground,
and just as
deep, grows
underground.
Our nest is
blessed to be
immense. It gives
us all a firm
defense, superior
to any fence. It
shields us from our
enemies. It keeps us
cooler, by degrees.
From floods and droughts
it guarantees. A prize
nobody will assign in
architectural design, but
still our hill suits us just fine.

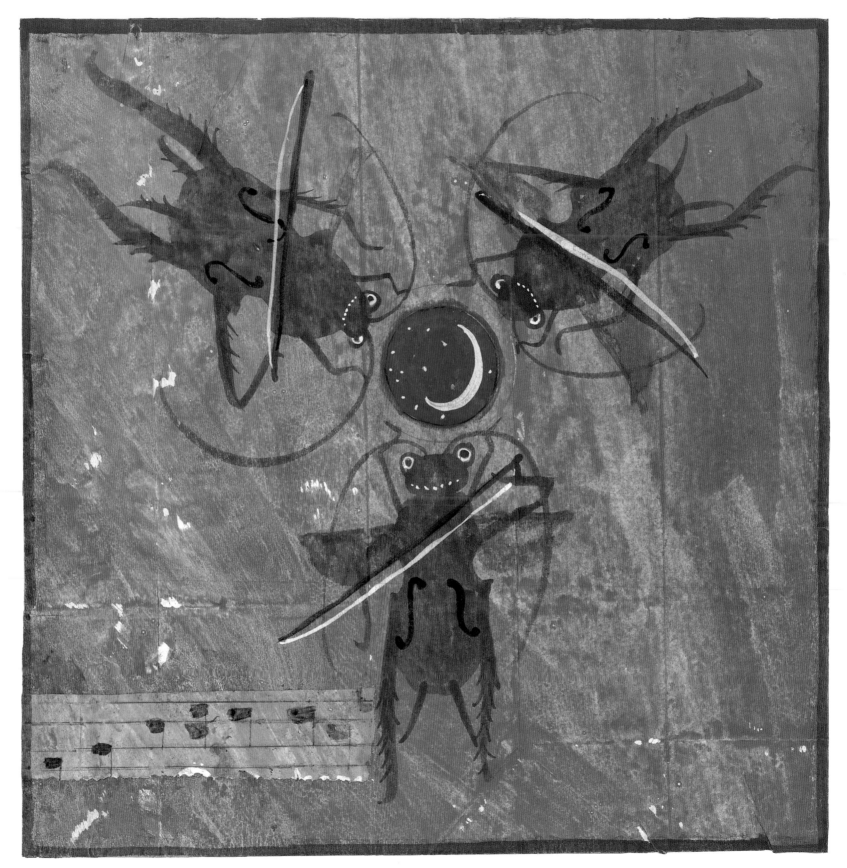

THE CRICKETS

You don't need tickets
To listen to crickets.
They chirp and cheep for free.
They fiddle and sing
By rubbing each wing,
And never will charge you a fee.

THE LOCUSTS

Hocus-
      pocus
We are locusts.
On your farm

We swarm,
We focus.
We choose to chew
Your grain,
Your grass.
They disappear
Each time we pass.

44

THE TICKS

Not gigan-tic.
Not roman-tic.
Not artis-tic.
Not majes-tic.
Not magne-tic.
Nor aesthe-tic.
Ticks are strictly parasi-tic.

THE MAYFLY

A mayfly flies
In May or June.
Its life is over
Far too soon.
A day or two
To dance,
To fly—
Hello
Hello
Good-bye
Good-bye.

The illustrations in this book were done in watercolor on
primed brown paper bags with collage.
The display type was set in Mason Alternate and Regular.
The text type was set in Sabon.
Color separations by Bright Arts, Ltd., Hong Kong
Printed by South China Printing Company, Ltd., Hong Kong
This book was printed on totally chlorine-free Nymolla Matte Art paper.
Production supervision by Stanley Redfern and Pascha Gerlinger
Designed by Kaelin Chappell